SIGNS OF LIFE...

OBSERVATIONS OF DEATH

Merry Christmas 2014

BY

CRAIG E. BETSON, RN, MHA

Vista
publishing, Inc.

COPYRIGHT © 1994 by Craig E. Betson

Edited by Susan Felice-Farese, MSN, RN, CS

Cover Design by Thomas Taylor of Thomcatt Graphics

Vista Publishing, Inc.
473 Broadway
Long Branch, NJ 07740
(908) 229-6500

This publication is designed for the reading pleasure of the general public. The author is solely responsible for the content of the written work and depicts the thoughts and emotions of the author.

Printed and bound in the United States of America

First Edition

ISBN: 1-880254-18-2

Library of Congress Catalog Card Number: 94-60686

U.S.A. Price	$9.95
Canada Price	$15.95

DEDICATION

This book is dedicated to *Roger and Margaret* who had the patience to wait for me to follow all the paths that brought me to this point.

To *Lynn*, who doesn't think I'm crazy as often anymore.

To *Maria*, facilitator of dreams, and the best nurse I know.

To *Richie*, *Beth*, and *Chase*. Where ever you went. I hope I helped you get there.

And to *Steve*, because every man needs a friend.

MEET THE AUTHOR

Craig E. Betson, RN, MHA

Born and raised in Knoxville, Tennessee, Craig acquired an avid love of the Great Smokey Mountains and the peacefulness found there. He earned a Geology degree from the University of Tennessee in 1981 and worked with the National Uranium Resource Evaluation crossing the country in search of uranium.

Craig also enjoyed restoring a home built in 1900 and started Fantasy Glass, a small stained glass business, that allowed him to travel to many local art shows.

While attending East Tennessee State University (1984-1986), working toward his BS in Nursing, Craig worked at Cherokee Adventures as a raft guide on the Nolochuky River. After graduating, he began his nursing career at East Tennessee Baptist Hospital on a medical-surgical wing. His career has given him the opportunity to gain experience in cardiovascular nursing, critical care nursing, and supervisory nursing.

Craig has recently earned his Masters in Healthcare Administration from the College of St. Francis.

He and his recent bride, Maria, also a nurse, live and work in Concord, Tennessee. They share a deep commitment and excitement of the nursing profession.

Craig has been writing poetry since high school. Even though he won a national poetry writing award, he never felt the need to save his poetry. Writing was a way to release the frustrations of every-day life. By writing down the emotions that were bothering him, the matter was resolved. The unique pressures of nursing school brought new insight into areas he had never dreamed of in life, or death. It was here that he began to collect his poetry into what was to become this book. *Signs of Life ... Observations of Death* is Craig's effort to help fellow nurses in conflict understand that they are not alone.

Craig feels that nurses will be the ones upon whom the health care system will rely as budgetary cuts force us to do more with less. It will be on the shoulders of the nurses who care to maintain quality care throughout the patient continuum. The stresses involved in this effort need to be brought out and validated. This is Craig's effort for validation for all nurses and their public.

TABLE OF CONTENTS

Preface

Section One: *My Poetry*

I Can	*1*
Night Watch	*2*
Secret Space	*3*
The Brass Ring	*4*
Bottled Water	*5*
When The Ghost Come Home	*6*
The Storm	*7*
The Passing	*8*
Hands On	*9*
Pick A Path	*10*
The Razor's Edge	*12*
Savanna, Ga.	*13*
The Chase	*14*
8/22/92	*15*
The Job	*16*
The Light	*17*
The Race	*18*
Trails End?	*19*
Walk The Line	*20*

Section Two: *In Dedication*

Just A Day	*22*
The Death	*24*
I Am A Nurse	*26*
Gut Feelings	*28*
To Touch A Fevered Brow	*30*

Section Three: *Dreaming*

Answers?	*33*
Dreamscape	*35*
Quiet Times	*36*
In Search Of A Dream	*37*
Silent Partner	*38*
Vision Quest	*39*

TABLE OF CONTENTS

Section Four: *Emotions*

    Emotion   *40*
    Does It All Come Down To This?   *42*
    Hello   *44*
    The Holocaust   *45*
    Hunter or Prey   *46*
    Keovorkian Dilemma   *47*
    Last One Out   *50*
    The Show   *52*
    Passing Touch   *53*
    When I Die   *54*

Section Five: *An Offering To True Love*

    Blue Denim   *56*
    My Will   *57*
    Do You Remember   *59*
    Flight   *61*
    The Time   *62*
    A Time For Dying   *63*

Section Six: *Thoughts And Reflections*

    Into The Abyss   *65*
    Reflections   *67*
    With A Bullet   *69*
    Daredevils   *71*
    Image   *73*
    What Is A Man   *74*
    Memories of Lesser Times   *75*
    Passages   *76*
    In Respect   *77*
    Death's A Puzzle   *78*
    The Noncompliant   *79*
    The Truth   *81*
    Time Passing   *82*
    What We Are   *83*
    Shells   *84*
    Woodstock Vaguely Remembered   *85*
    Freedom   *86*

Conclusion   *87*

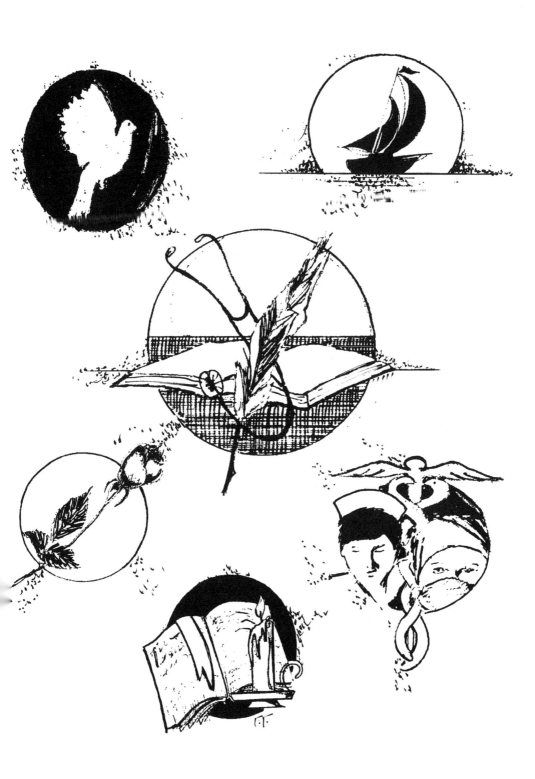

Preface

Nursing is a career which draws many different people for varied reasons. I was drawn to nursing because it was the only place where I felt that on a daily basis I could make a difference. Graduating from East Tennessee State University in May of 1986, I started employment at East Tennessee Baptist Hospital. I was sure I had the knowledge to be in control of all situations that I was to come in contact with. Six years later, all I'm sure of is that whenever I get sure of myself, some situation presents which lets me know that I'm still learning. I imagine that's part of the intensity of emotions required of a good nurse. It is quite demanding.

This book is a small offering of what we go through on an almost daily basis. It is an attempt to portray on paper how it feels to have your patient die on you. For those that have not experienced it, it is an event that you cannot help but take personally. The unvoiced demands, responsibility, and workload can, at times, be more than the most seasoned nurse can carry alone. These stories go out to them. From the Emergency Room to the Intensive Care Unit to the floor patients, all have their particular demands and stresses. I have tried to voice some of the emotions that I felt working as a floor nurse, then to ICU, and finally as a supervisor of ICU. Not all of these feelings are hopeful, nor are they pretty. I hope that I can make you understand just a small portion of what I have laid out on paper. What drives us to be, and what makes us work.

Welcome to my world.

SECTION ONE

My Poetry

I CARE

We have discovered
what we know as
the truth. The Healers
are meant to save lives.
And that is how
it should be - as we've
been told. Now we are
forced to assess the
scene in a different
light, a little darker.
Free health care
to all who ask.
But is that not
essentially what we
have. The poor,
the traumatized,
the ignored. All
deserve care. A
sane and noble
gesture. But what
of the causes of
these people?
Ignorance, hatred,
racism, abuse,
drugs. Do we
really have a
chance against them?
For we must first
address the cause
for the people without
a home, a family,
a job. Before we can
begin to heal the sores,
cure the cause.
Treating symptoms.
For the symptoms of
the diseases of
humanity are the
wounds of man.

11/12/93

Night Watch

I am your healer, servant
contact with the world.
So I tell you what I see
in life outside, in me.
And hope some cells of
what you were can hear
What I say at night
while the world sleeps
we talk.
I hope you're listening.
In either case the motions
ease my worry
and my ineffectualness.
For you may die
despite my acts,
but it will not be
because of them.
This is my pledge.
All I have to offer
is my pride
in my profession
and my best.
For if the roles
were reversed,
I could only hope
the same from you.

04/87

Secret Space

Pause in the garden
Introspective time
And my parameters
begin to shrink
A barrier against
that which buffets
my mind, my self.
To feel air, the sun,
brush my senses.
So I expand
in the smaller
space

The Brass Ring

I have often wandered
on this slow parade of life.
Through parodies, fantasies,
laughter, feelings, strife.
And wondered where I go.

To ride the wheel, feeling high
my heart slid in my pocket.
Captured pictures, under glass
caught beneath a locket.
And wondered what I know.

Hit the round astride my horse,
caught the steady canter.
Try to gaze unto the face
and just maintain the banter.
And wondered what I show.

The dazzle lights of tinseltown
all lure into the swell.
Caramel corn and popcorn salt
is a call I know too well.
I hope the high is not too low.

09/15/89

Bottled Water

Bottled water,
what a concept!
From the states
over to Europe,
and from Europe
over here. Seek
what you lack.
Just look behind
but don't look back.
It makes the future
not quite black.
It still sparkles
on the cracks.

12/18/91

5

When The Ghost Come Home

A patient complimented me today.
A healthy one now. Secure
in the fact that I was watching.
In battle men trust one another
with their lives on action alone.
A decision that you are safe.
And they are safe for the night.
What was the deciding factor?
What creates that secure feeling?
Patient approach, time spent,
tone of voice, touch, eye contact.
All the things a person does.
But which did I do that turned
the key of security for you.
That is the puzzle.
For the features only change
in marginal ways. The drapes,
the paint, call lights and beds.
So try and fit the pieces into
the person and seek what
they really need. When all
external stressors are removed,
the body heals much faster.

05/30/94

The Storm

We went to war today.
Justified or not, we breach
a line not passed
in memory better than
pictures. Ill thought
videos from hell.
Vietnam just missed.
A coincidence of birth
allowed my passage,
between frames. All
I can see is the waste.
Bodies we fight to keep
are sent to the most
technologic killing zone
man has yet devised.
I care not for the
illustration, or the effect.
All I see are ruins.
The waste of lives,
of dreams of men.
Must we destroy lives
for an unsound ideology
formed by the business
of the lives we assume
are necessary to us.
We all created this.

01/16/91

The Passing

Sometimes I am overcome
by the events surrounding me.
What some visualize as an
avoidable event, to some
extent, I see daily.
All this hype about death
is so overstated. The initial
point of "code" is so powerful.
The surge of adrenalin, the
frantic activity, all paced
by an iridescent line. Our
least visible, but most obvious
enemy. Alas, we cannot reverse
the abuse of years in minutes.
The voices become quieter,
the flurry slows as methods fail.
The drips are running, the meds
are in. The cells not wishing
to respond, in defeat, we
accept our own mortality.

1/91

HANDS ON

Hands On, I believe they
called it in school
I've come to feel that
it is a time of cleansing.
If I can lead the broken
away from me, washed,
in a sense. Then, the
course was taken complete.
In body, if not in spirit.

12/90

Pick a Path

The train clicked softly against the rails
Silver moonlight caressed her face at rest.
Gentle rocking of the cars as night passes.
The past slipping with the miles beneath,
beneath that which is allowed to be seen.

Fertile garden tended by one, badly.
The plants sicken, those visible to the eye.
Thus the fruit born scarred and rotted.
Picked none the less by the harvesters.
Weeders of the weak. Seeking food.

The roughness of the starched cloth,
Silken gown against the skin, brushed.
Tactile growth extends as sight turns
soft shades of greys and black, blurred.
Yet distinct in image. Rememberances.

Why do the colors still come in the dark?
Soft and pleasing loses taste in starkness.
Runaway screams a doppler of terror.
Yet can the taste of fear diminish time?
The grey is running away with the spoon.

The whistle brings the consciousness back.
Abrupt termination of thought process.
To only flesh and blood with inherent
aches and pains, day to day, life.
The rocking slowly stops. Placement.

Interference in the chain of action.
What makes us wander to the edge,
seek what we know will destroy us.
Careening headlong plunge down.
Into the face of dreams and screams.

Brakes squeal with frictions turn.
The lurch as cars compact to stop.
Loudspeakers blurrily blare information.
To the unknowing, and the unwilling.
The window cool to the cheek, soothing.

A wanderer along life's single path.
Some allow it to be a row.
Just rowed corn waving at the wind.
The weaker stalks not quite reaching,
falling with the weight born, not carried.

The station bustles with passing sights.
Destinations known. But the whistle
breaks through, once more in time.
So the trek to peace is never begun.
Fear once more denies that once sought.

06/09/94

The Razor's Edge

Stately tread is postured, slow.
Criminal fear, imperfect show.
Gradual shift in planetary terms.
Of ordination
and velocity. To triangulate
the chose course, interspatially.
Now, without remorse.
Lights and shadow
shrink to fit. As reality,
and the spin, internalize.
An extrapolation of what
can be, from what is.
So the orientation
becomes acutely vertical
in a planar sense.
Thus to walk
the razors edge.

01/02/93

Savannah, Ga.

Days Inn
at a table
by a coke bottle
with some change,
and keys. Oops,
and a bottle cap.
Messy, messy!
Good help is hard
to find. They take
the change, and leave
the bottle.

04/19/90

The Chase

I have followed
what you portray
as the truth.
Foolish dreamer.
Incomplete schemer
in a whirl of color
and dream whiplash
For you see me.
All I seek to be
catch me fool
don't let me spool
reel of fear.
Play yet again the fool
as idle demons play
across my eyes.
Subtle mind rewind.
And again I'm behind
that which I sought
more than what I've bought
Returns to haunt me.
Fills all I can see
all the sound within me
shatters what I touch.
Do I seek too much?
So the pulse bounds
carotid sounds
of life on board.
Twin edge sword.
For the cord
strikes a note
not felt in ages,
ruffled pages.

Books undisturbed
by adjectives, or verbs,
literary pace, or space.
Cross my face.
Visions dreamed
Dreams unseamed
to cascade upon me.
Sweet rain of truth.
Visions blessed,
the cord unstressed
by weight, or sanctity.
All we see,
And the entity still grows despite
what we do for it,
or against it.

08/22/92

The Job

I've known you for over three months
and I've never heard you speak.
I never really thought you would
have the opportunity. To watch
the fear in your eyes fade as the
drugs we gave took effect. So we
could slip the tubes in place to
let you breathe, eat, and drain
yourself of poisons. To give us
time to fight the symptoms, and
the chemistries to maintain that
which we accept as ideal for life.
And you beat the odds. Mentally
and physically you are intact.
A true symbol of what we are.
To save and improve lives. I have
never heard a sound so sweet
as the sound of your voice.
It carries the ring of victory.

02/04/93

16

The Light

Watch the steamy summer sweat
Rivulet swarm, wringing wet.
Lazy buzz, crickets sing
birds fly by on listless wing.
Leaves curl under, break to touch
all consumed by summer's touch.
Leaves seek light and find too much
powdered earth can't yield as such.
Waters glisten has not blessed
Mouths of God wrought confess
On the millions of this trees.

07/88

The Race

Life's simple tread
breaks stride,
And I am left
fumbling with
the laces.
In a slow motion
picture of failure.
The important
the most important
race I've run
is sideswiped
by my mind.
The race momentarily
Halted. Rained out.

06/90

18

Trails End?

Will we ever wander on,
carry our unfinished wings?
In some protected place
concealed behind the face
that we decide to show.
And when the colors
start to run,
Lose the knowledge
of the sun.
Count the fall
starting gun
for the end
has begun.
Sunsets fine,
tenuous glow.
Strive for light,
miss the show.
Seek light
in dark rooms.
Bound dressing
over wounds
that ooze,
forever fresh.
Tattered soul
starts to mesh
with the visions
that we seek.

2/15/92

Walk The Line

Our work came back
to us today. A living
representation of what
we are about. I had
often wondered, after
the months you
stayed in the unit,
where life had led you.
Months of care,
from the excellent,
to the mediocre.
To give you what?
A little more time
on this sphere
of earth. You are
truly a million
dollar man, and
a lucky one at that.
What were the odds
that you beat? What is the
destiny you
have to fulfill? For
surely some purpose
is ordained for
you. Do you remember
the night that I
spent more time
than I had preparing
you for the day
I felt you would
surely die? I hope
not, but I do.
I laid my hand
in yours and
said goodbye.
But you fooled
me, and others,

for you lie in
front of me.
Are we reaching
a time when
dollars would
have decided
your fate?
Failure to thrive
would have doomed
you. On whose
head will this
call lie? Some
inpersonal
voice on a line,
and a dial tone.
For in our need
to supply care
to all, those that
walk the line
will come up short.
In dollars, if not
life. In any case,
it's good to see
you. For I can look
back on my actions,
and my care and
realize that I helped
bring you to this
point in your life,
so much better
than what you
had been offered.

10/11/93

SECTION TWO

In
Dedication

Being a man and acquiring a ready made family
is a difficult thing to do. No more difficult than
trying to accept a stranger into your home I imagine.
Things that need to be learned are sometimes rushed,
or misunderstood. This was written on an outing together.
A learning of mutual capabilities, respect, and trust. A
learning day for what family is supposed to be about,
at least from our varied viewpoints. A day for broadened
perspectives.

This is dedicated to Tripp and Landon.

Just a Day

Death by degrees
Intrinsic fees
that are left behind.
A day at the sea.
Seemingly pleased,
but not really sure.
Was the day wasted?
To be out, away,
from that which we
define as space, today.
The boundaries of what
you knew as men
expanded while I watched.
As close to a father as
I'll ever be. Know,
that I love you.
I want you to be
what you dream.

Pursue your dreams.

7/31/94

This poem is dedicated to Pat Basler, RN.

On one night that was particularly stressful,we lost a patient that was terminal. A young patient that still seemed brimming with unfulfilled dreams. Not like the overdosed,voluntarily seeking an end. She wanted life and all it had to offer. The tension afterwards was palpable,all our training was for naught. This was my way of apologizing to Pat for being unable to say or do that which was required at the time.

We seldom get second chances.

THE DEATH

A patient died tonight.
Not the usual,
but someone we had
come to know
Special in her trust
of us.
Did we let her down?
A disservice
In watching her go
doing nothing
Doing what we were
trained to do
Or did we help her
to a better place?
A place beyond life
and pain. No matter,
she has travelled
from us, to beyond.
I feel your pain
inside me.
That point of crying
unrelieved. The ache
just builds, there is
no release.
I want to touch, to
hold you, and share
my pain with yours.
I can see it in
your eyes, but I fear
the gesture - misconstrued.
So I hold my pain
deep inside,
And it burns me.

*Unreleased, I hide
my feeling in abruptness.
Reviewing the moments
passed, events shared.
The burden becomes
too great to carry.
Pride no longer
becomes me.
Do we fall? Lost
in ourselves, alone?
A burden shared, carried
a lighter load.
For both parties, afraid
to offer weakness. But what
better strength than numbers?*

Far stronger than me.

04/10/90

I Am A Nurse.

I am a complex person
a parody of dreams.
A shock of white, with reason,
not quite what it seems.
So ask me any question
I'll temper it with truth
I remember every lesson
and can quote it back, forsooth.
But to the docs we're blind
assessments are suspect
their words may be unkind,
we don't get no respect.
And the families, oh the families,
well we just make them leave.
We're just there for tea and cookies
like they saw on the TV.
But none of that is really me
and it's sure not why I do this.
I see no roles I'd like to play
in any of "those" movies.
Just what my patient sees in me
That's my starring role.
It's in their face that I can see
the picture of my soul.

09/86

26

I went and worked at a rural hospital today. Four bed unit, how tough can this be I thought to myself. Just a monitor for the old heart rate and a dynamap for the blood pressure. It doesn't get any better than this, No swan ganz, arterial lines, pulse oximeter none of those irritating alarms that I take for granted back in my home unit. Alarms that tell me information that I am so used to hearing that they become background noise. I don't even realize I am absorbing the information for the most part, but I have come to rely upon that peripheral information to make patient assessments. It is so easy to rely on machines and ignore the person that you are really taking care of that is lying in the bed. Touch, feel, absorb what the patient is telling you without ever saying a word. This is what nursing is all about and I've gotten rusty. I helped work up a patient in the ER that was very ill. I then admitted him to the unit since I was only orienting to the ER. Within an hour, the patient had V-tach, loss of blood pressure, respiratory arrest, intubation, cardioversion, and death. People die just as quick out here too. It was truly a learning experience for me. The camaraderie of the people that worked there had let me know that the way they feel about their patients is just the same as the way I feel about mine. Protective, caring, loving each our own way. The feeling of a team working together for the common good was wonderful. This poem goes to out to Roane County Baptist Hospital and all the fine folks that work there.

Gut Feelings

Patient assessment.
What does that really entail?
Is it the history? List of sins,
list of faults, errors in programming,
A log of survival for many. Fools.
Anyone can see the scars of life on you.

Family infrastructure.
Could the secret lie in that?
What style of support system
do you have? Strong, concerned,
participatory family that cares for you.
Or the usual, the distant relative's phone?

Survival time.
That's what it's about.
What will increase or decrease
your block of time with me here,
now, in this room? If I guess wrong,
about what is pertinent, you will die.

So feel.
I feel for you in there.
Where are you in there dammit?
A silent tachycardic lump.
And I have to fix not the symptoms,
but the cause or you will surely die by me.

The monitor
feeds me bits of information.
Tattletale of a system in chaos.
Blood pressure falling, respirations
falling, temperature falling, intubation.
Alarm bells of a final shutdown imminent.

The Edge,
crossed over for you.
I can feel it when you crossed.
I knew it, but I had to give you chances.
Chances to live today, but you didn't keep
your part of the bargain. You died today.

The line
has been pushed back next time.
For you see the learning has occured.
You who have nothing now, are teaching me.
So the next time, should you ever come back,
you will survive. Gut feelings always take you home.

06/05/94

TO TOUCH A FEVERED BROW

The smallest patient I've ever had for her age.
Eighty pounds of spunk wrapped in frail body.
Trying to deny that she is really sick, just weak.
So I think of what I would look at if She was,
mine. So I straighten her and fluff the pillow.
Pull down tight the sheet, adjust the gown,
comb the hair. All the things we do when
we are well. And can do for ourselves.

Often I really wonder if anyone but me cares.
Why do I really go in the room to explain,
when a call from the desk will do? Extra.
Extra time, steps, responsibility, duties.
But that is the way I have learned.
To know that with the patient, inevitable,
one call out will count. The odds are
against us in the long run. I'm in.

The lab tech draws the q4 hr. hematocrit.
The strangest look upon his face.
As he gazes at the woman I have spent
thirty minutes fixing and fussing with.
To think that perhaps no one would care.
And says, "She looks just like my grandmother."
Thus the cascade of reactions to my actions.
A finger flick to dew laden grass cascades
a shower of comfort, and care to others.

Because we all evaluate the patients we see.
The alarms that go off in other nurses rooms.
An instant evaluation of the information seen.
The patient's color, respiration, position, eyes.
Monitor patterns, causes for disturbance, fault
checking in an evaluation of what is in, and out,
of place. The columns don't add up, and time,
is taken from the allotted slot for something else.

Adjustments as priorities shift. What can wait?
What must I do, who is around? What can we
use? Fault finding and resource evaluation.
The tasks are rearranged, the patients breath.
The pattern improves. And the family is with
my patient, the little lady. And she still looks
just like I left her. So the family talks and is
friendly. Because they can see I care. Response.

7/2/94

31

SECTION THREE

Dreaming

Depression is a demon
that chases all nurses. It
takes may forms, and
labels. "Burn-out", is the
most often used term and
it adequately describes
how you feel when events
overwhelm the senses. I
have a strong belief in
God. I have seen too
many unexplainable
things occur. The patient
that would not die until
the wife, husband, or
child came to see them.
The person that against
all odds walked away
from the crash without a
scratch. Unexplainable
things that make us lie
awake in bed at night and
talk, while we hope
someone is listening.
This was written on one
of those nights, and I
believe someone listened.

Answers?

God,
Can we talk?
As I stare at a wall
seeking dimensions of dreams
for this ache within my soul.
Speak,
to me
a pandemonium
of a mindflow of hurt
pours from my soul to you.
Wait,
for me.
Be ever patient
for my spirit is weak
and my colors ever varied.
Accept,
my apology
for my variance.
My vacillations in strength
are great, as are my weaknesses.
Listen,
to me.
Just me a moment
for I have no one else
that will wipe my gathered tear.
Trust,
that I
do mean this
The promises unkept
and this you know, but give.

Believe,
I do
believe in you
for I can feel you
Touch you with my mind.
Think,
as I
dwell on you
Is a prayer required?
or is the dream within me
Enough?

04/19/90

Dreamscape

Welcome to my place
lights beckon space,
My place of dreams
not all as it seems.
For in the scene
so crystal clean
Is my heart.
Just the start
sensory reel.
Touch my eyes
sweet surprise.
Visions mingle,
not I single
but the pair
can you snare
What I am?

04/14/91

Quiet Times

Solitude.
I can think back
to when it was
a punishment.
Now,
a commodity,
to be traded
or even given.
Time,
trickles through
the fingers of
foolish youth.
Streams
past the timid,
missed chances,
fading views.
Burns,
as the devil
consuming
all of us.

So,
what of time
spent alone.
Is it wasted?
Sought?
or really found.
Garnered pebbles
from the stream.
Held,
or at least
imagined held,
by the mind.
Lost,
but never sought.
Found, but
never dreamed
Escape,
into the silence,
to be delivered
to oneself.

4/10/94

In Search of a Dream

What is this thing
that I've become?
A reactionary being
in part to you, in part,
to what I was. An offering
to what I thought was needed.
Yet I don't know you.
What you need, want, seek.
Am I already what you need
and try to change to what
I am used to. Old habits
die hard. An unending
stream of experiences
in life's flow. For someday
we may fail. Our expectations
lacking in depth. Not what
we sought, but what we found.
Which is what we expected,
all along.

12/02/92

Silent Partner

Walked a dream
came unseamed
close parameter
Love it seems
foundered schemes
of what I am.
Singular, as it
were. Myself.
A dream revisited,
captured by me
and lost. Vistas
missed, favored kiss
slips away. Savored.
Never change,
rearranged to suit.
The fixtures
grasp me, as I am.
Once again
come to terms
in a dream

04/18/92

Vision Quest

The day dawns
fresh with miracles
to be discovered
and wondered at.
The glint of sun
touches your hair
as vision expands
to become aware.
All that is beside,
inside my heart
creates new dreams.
Contemplations of
what is, what can be.
Imagination the
only qualifier.
An unlimited
scope of the world
expands before us.
A beckoning light.
A beacon reaching,
searching for dreamers.
Frustrated by the
lack of vision
the night has held.

9/24/92

SECTION FOUR

Emotions

Emotion

What is the tie that binds?
Fiery burn to slow unwind.
Tender touch to stinging tears
sudden onslaught of our fears.

If to wish upon a star,
Verbal onslaught to a car,
pride that goes before the storm,
hair that grows beyond the norm.

Emotion drives in all these things.
Fastest cars and golden rings.
So all our demons persue us
just as the others revue us.

Pride in doses all can swallow
in noble deeds, not so hollow,
is just and well received.
But it must be believed.

Fear can spur to greater height.
Far surpass just common might.
Or bury us in ineptitude,
cast us out in solitude.

Exhileration on endorphines
jumping out of aeroplanes,
just to feel the rush.
Before the final push.

Love is the most sought,
the one that can't be bought.
The one we all seek,
the prideful and meek.

Some take it, or leave,
some only seek to grieve.
For those that got away.
So how to make it stay?

Have pride in what you do.
To yourself be true.
You plant the seeds
for words behind deeds.

Use fear as your tools
to bypass the fools
found dead for a call
none seem to recall.

Life is a journey.
Birth to a gurney.
What happens between
is yet to be seen.

You will find what you sow.
More or less than you owe.
For your heart shows more
than you know.

04/19/94

Does it all come down to this?

I saw you in the hallway
leaning against a wall
Just passed in a moment
but I know you've lost it all.
Did it find your husband?
daughter or son?
Endgame of a lifetime
you thought would never end.
It just all seems so unfair
they had so much to give.
A thousand wishful promises
if only they could live.
So we worked upon the body
the drugs did run their course,
just to trap the person
inside a living corpse.
So they blink to say
"I love You"
or did they move at all.
Try to feel more positive
as you walk back down the hall.
Say you did the right thing
we brought them back for you.
Say they're in there somewhere
And it just won't seem so cruel.

01/90

42

Working in a nursing home prior to my education as a nurse was probably the most difficult job I have ever had. The role of maintainer instead of a healer is very difficult. To see people on a daily basis that you cannot help but become attached to, and that you also know will eventually die there, was extremely difficult. This is a story about the repetitiveness of the days, the basic functions performed, and the emotions involved.

Welcome to Sam's world.

Hello

Hello Sam!
Are you with us today?
It's eight AM and
breakfast
is ready. Do you know
what day it is?
Scrambled eggs again
and some sausage too.

Hello Sam!
Visitors today?
No, sorry.
No one will come
to match your stare.
Eat your lunch now.

Hello Sam!
What thoughts lie
behind your clouded
eyes?
Memories unreeling,
edit
Fast forward of days
numbing in similarity.

Hello Sam!
Are you in pain?
Blink once for yes
Take communion.
Let the pain, reality
slip away.

Hello Sam!
Bodies in the
lobby
Parked in the sun
Feeble attempt
to cleanse the
mind
You're wearing
dinner.
I see.

07/15/85

The Holocaust

A single death
unnoticed in the eddy
Flash of silver
dulling with the wash,
then swirling past.
A pretence of life.
In all of its
inconsequentiality
Gave notice, warning
of the greater sickness
that was spreading.
To engulf. The water
runs on, ever clear
to the passive observer.
The depth, clarity
never changes, just
the toxin carried.
Till days past without
even the dullest glint
of life that was
within. The only sin
was inactivity, failure
to act, in defense,
in time. Are we
any less at fault
if we allow or caused
the death.

09/09/92

Hunter or Prey

Acrid smell of gunpowder still lingers
as does the ringing of the shots.
A sound to send chills through
the bravest of men.
The sudden spray of death.
Familiar from movies
and the good guy never,
well hardly ever, dies.
But the man with the gun
decides your role in this.
Unwilling passenger on
a shakey flight in time.
In warp time, decide.
Live or die in seconds.
Are we destined to become
numb to this also.
As our senses become blunt
from the onslaught TV brings.
Corpses in the river,
bodies on the highway,
soldiers learning to die.
News to us.
Misery sells.
Say confession
for the camera.

    Smile

7/94

46

Kevorkian Dilemma

If I had a dog
that could not walk,
could not speak,
could not eat,
I would kill it.
Farm raising
some would blame.
But I see it not
as a punishment
or as a cruelty.
But as a final
statement of love.
I love you enough
to let you go.
The ultimate
unselfish act.
You are taken
from my life.
Is that not what
Kevorkian is saying?
He has taken
people who will
die and given
them a gift.
What better
choice in life
than to say goodbye
and leave this world
without pain or fear.
Do we all not make
this choice daily.
The small deaths
of relationships,
and interactions.
You decide what
will blossom

and grow. Yet at
 the big question
we choke. Afraid
that if we give
away that power,
someone else will
decide for us.
And those anger
for the power
invade us from
without. None
are safe from
the random
bullet. Natural
selection in a
random form.
Upraised hand
to shield a storm.

11/12/93

This poem is probably the strongest in relation to me due to the contrast it held. To walk into a room with this beautiful scene, and know that there is death right behind the door. A woman had decided to let her husband die without intubation, a merciful choice because we would most likely watch him die some time later still on the ventilator. The intensity of the emotions in the room still wash over me whenever I read or think about this. The decision was right, the time was right, but the effects are no less shattering. To hold a hand, wipe a tear, give a hug, sometimes that is all we are powerful enough to do. Many times it is not enough for the family member or the nurse.

Last One Out

I watched you gazing
out the window
Bathed in sunbeams
golden light
Diamond glistens
sparkle bright
Dust motes spun
daytime starlight
of a dream.

Listen as your mate
breathes his last
Where is your future
Alone?
Childhood dreams
foreshortened
in a span
of minutes
Time flown.

You've decided
that he passes
from this world
beyond, infinite smile
flash of time
from together
to alone
Too strong
to cope

Overpowered
and defenseless
You're defenseless
with the onslaught
Of emotions
and dread
You see.
Where you are.
What you are.

A Mrs. with
no man
In a sea of
the more than
You have lost
are last
In a race
with no winner
Can you tie?

Wish to die?

The last one out.

06/12/87

The Show

I watched a movie today
events experienced, never felt.
A progression of ideals of man
and I wonder at my fate.
Will I become cynical, a disbeliever?
For what is the point of lost ideals.
Could the well be too deep,
too chaotic to be freed from.
At times reality slips from my grasp
the darkness seems all consuming.
Then I must believe in my sanity,
in my family, in my heart,
for that is all I hold true
honest and strong to me.
For who shall know of me
when I am less than photographs
and remembered places to them.
Can I touch you? Help you?
Help you to be what you will be
and will you think of me?

05/12/86

Passing Touch

First the flower
then the stone
truth to light
we die alone

In tender arms
too cold touch
to beyond harms
reach as such

Words we offer
distant dreams
see the coffer
of your schemes

For the moment
we are touched
by the torment
visions rushed

Cry my friend
let them past
because the end
will never last

01/14/92

When I Die

Speaking of me
past death's cries
I wish to see
with kitten's eyes.
All is new
full of wonder,
Sadly mew
over blunder
And carry on
moments past
Cat regrets
never last

10/18/90

SECTION FIVE

An Offering To True
LOVE

"Blue Denim" is my offering to true love. To find that one person that makes life complete is a search that many never complete. I felt blessed to have found that person that makes me feel that way. To describe the emotion is an altogether different challenge. What substance, what feeling could describe the power contained in a touch? Forgiveness, Love, sorrow, all in the touch of a hand, the brushing touch of a kiss. What can draw you into that safe sense of security better than a worn pair of jeans. Comfort breeds familiarity.

Blue Denim

We are the loose threads,
the wayward ones. Not following
the measured tread.
Sillian ties from cotton thread
bind us close, blind th, wind
Till we die - can it be?
Could it be some simple words
could cleave our souls
in the bond unbreakable.
It is simpler, far simpler
to feel than do, chosen few
ever feel, even steel to bind.

Touch me, feel my strength.

Weavers touch subtle unwind.
The failing of the knot,
to seek the perfect fit.
Soft caress, a favored jean
silken shadows touch
comfort in familiarity.
So owning is being owned
because it is comfort
and the best of safe places.

Touch me, feel my need.

The sun touches me.
Silhouettes two threads
bound by light, to be free.
So enjoy the day, the time,
with me, in you, by you
and yet I need you more.

Touch me, feel my mind.

The threads drift down
so close, yet so apart.
Wish to be inside me.

Touch me, feel me.

04/12/87

56

My Will

Think of me in love? Trust?
and know that I showed you
my secrets, my dreams, my will.
Please use them to become
what you are in your dreams.
In you I live forever

04/24/91

I think that an abnormally
high percentage of nurses
are divorced. I'm not
sure it it's due to the
awareness of passing
time, or the independent
nature of the person
attracted to the field.
This is a passage of life,
and love through growing
up. We all constantly
change and grow,
relationships being a part
of this growth. So we
metamorphosize to
become what we seek, or
at least what we think we
seek. This is an
acknowledgment of
change and all it allows
us to become.

Do you Remember?

Do you remember the days
of the old school yard?
We used to laugh,
we used to sing.
We found such wonder
in the old school yard.
Laughed in the sun
life was such fun.
Remember the laughter
of the old school yard?

Do you remember me?

Remember the days
of the old high school?
We used to laugh
we used to love.
We lost some wonder
in the old high school
Learned how to hurt
and how to cry
To lose first love
in the old high school.

Do you remember me?

Can you remember the days
of the college town?
We used to laugh,
we used some friends.
We learned to drink
in college town.
Learned to say
I love you
when we meant
I'll take you.

Do you remember me?

Do you remember the days
of married life?
We used to laugh,
we used to lie.
We lost all love
in married life
How to cry,
and fantasize.
While we cry.
Alone.

Do you remember me?

Remember the day
you find true love.
You will laugh,
you can play.
Find the wonder
of true love.
Laugh in the sun,
Life is such fun
Remember the laughter
of true love.

We'll wait and see.

Flight

Strive
To be free
Join the birds
in the sky
and learn
how to fly
Then,
Reach down
and touch someone
With Love.

03/73

The Time

Starlight haze
slowly fades
in the shimmer
of a new day.
And I wish you were here.
Not because of the scene,
but the feeling of sharing.
The moment, the space.
For my best times
are our times.
The moments we share
are forever.

08/10/89

A Time For Dying

I watched your mother die tonight,
While I just laid my hand
upon your shoulder. No running
feet, no call of code, no panicked
meds. Just a quiet sob at a darkened
bedside with a lifetime of untold
"I Love You" pouring out. So I give
reassurance that letting her go is
the right thing to do. That if it
was my mother that I would do
the same. How do you train for this?
How better to prepare my psyche
to support the family, the patient,
and the nurse. What is the priority
at the time? And how best to serve.
Much less to resolve what I feel
while carrying on the act.

01/26/93

SECTION SIX

Thoughts & Reflections

I work in a cardiovascular surgical unit. We recover immediate post-operative open heart patients. This is one of the most rewarding parts of being a nurse to me. To take someone that looks almost dead on arrival, and make them a living, viable, human being. Who is this person that I know from a sheet of information and some interaction with their family. How do I interpret their needs, and rank them in importance with the other priorities that I have. Can I depend on them doing what I tell them to do when I need them to do it. Will they breath deeply when they need to? Will they sit up and cough with enough effort too actually do something? Will they try to relax so I don't have to give them drugs? Sort of like a maestro leading a symphony, we lead this one person to the land of perfect numbers. Hemodynamically stable with a cardiac output grater than 2.3, heart rate less then 100 but greater than 60, respiratory rate around 20bpm, the perfect human. To come from such poor working materials at times. But at seven AM, the truth comes out, in black and white, in order. It is so easy to just look at the technical aspect of the job, to get caught up in the numbers, and forget that there is a living human on the end of all those cables and tubes. Some of the people are used to being dependent on others because of their disease process. Valve replacements tend to be this way because the process has usually evolved to where they are weaker than most others and therefore more reliant on others care. The acute myocardial infarction, the failed percutaneous transluminal coronary angioplasty. These are the fearful, the unprepared for coping with a situation that they neither understand or want. The Abyss is about working with someone that is unprepared for the surgery. Bringing them from the anesthetic haze of fears and dreams back to the reality of living. Teaching them to rely on themselves once more as the responsibilities of life begin their insistent demands.

Into The Abyss

I saw where you went tonight.
Into the Abyss, that's where.
Why did you take me?
I don't want to see you,
like that, you know?
But we went anyway.
I saw the look when
the anesthetic wore off,
the first time. Where
did you go? I saw
the fear in your eyes.
You came around,
a tangle of tubes,
lines and wires.
To be disassembled,
reanimated to return,
to live with us. God
gave us this gift.
Informed consent,
such that it is.
Because none of
the choices seemed
to fit this case.
But the point should have
never been reached.
And so for a while,
I carried you.
Your debt to the
World, such as you,
consider it a little
in the minus column.
I watch as you struggle to breath.
Your face crimson,
your eyes wide,
fists clenched tight.
Gaging how bad
we need to remove

the offending item
versus what you
can endure.
Pain medicine
versus need to
ventilate, be alert.
Pressures of time,
demands of doctors,
need for speed.
All factors in how
your personal
experience will go.
How sick is my
other patient, the
one you'll never see.
Or care about for that
matter. For this is
your trip. Tied up
and no place to go,
but inside.
Personal demons.
Thoughts of pride.
Thoughts of death.
Thoughts of revenge.
So hate or love me,
you still will be here
come morning.
Probably only thankful
that I moistened
your lips so often.
Close resemblance
to a mother's kiss.
The first final proof
you had left the Abyss.

02/16/94

Reflections

I sat by a stream
and wondered
This, in all
its simplicity
unappreciated
goes on forever.
A simple gurgle.
Water passing rocks,
such as I
a mere rock.
Deflecting the flow
of lives
around me,
eventually I too
will wear away.
Bits and pieces
passed downstream
from my life.
Can I touch you,
help you build?
On the solid ground
of your life?
Or merely drift,
flotsam in the
stream of life.

9/26/90

When a code is called in the emergency room, it means that they have encountered something that even their capable hands were not prepared to deal with. On a fairly quiet night in the unit, I responded to a code in the emergency room. A strong, healthy looking fifteen year old boy was laid out on the table. The only evidence of trouble besides the frantic efforts was the small hole in his chest, the size of a 22 caliber bullet. After furious efforts to maintain blood pressure and pulse, the chest was opened to discover the bullet had passed through the ventricle of the heart leaving a large hole with no hope of repair. the realization that we were so limited in help to someone that appeared so healthy hit me very hard. Then the senselessness of it all struck home. Was it drugs, a girl, family, or money that caused the trigger to be pulled? Somehow all excuses seem to pale in the light of day, and reason.

With A Bullet

Flurried efforts slow decline
lust to absorb it missed that
Manual pace across the screen
A trace of life in emerald green
Shouted orders, running steps
Cried remorse with shared regrets
Someones life is fading fast
The only future is their past
So what of things they had not done?
Glory earned or honors won
What of honors still unachieved
Unspoken truths never believed?
Lips try to move, to form a voice
Compression down removes the choice
And so the eye begins to glaze
Slack expression turns the face
Into the mask of failure

10/20/92

69

After watching an absurd bit about stuntmen on television one night, I thought about how little of the event was actually left to chance. Ramp angles calculated with precise timing and speeds. The effect was dramatic enough, but was anything actually left to chance? Working as a nurse is what I see as the most daring profession. The direct admit off of a MedFlight helicopter is more exciting than any stunt. Anxious glances to see some glimpse of what you may be getting coming down the hall. In a matter of minutes, the information is transferred to you and the responsibility becomes yours to keep this person that you know nothing about alive. Heart rate, blood pressure, lung sounds, breathing rate, pain, all assessed in a matter of minutes. Observation and knowledge may be the only thing between life and death for this patient, this person, that you just met. A long shift of hard work lies ahead for a reward of being able to go home on time at the end of the shift Maybe a thank you, if you're lucky. Yet we go home knowing that, a least in the one room, that person was as safe as you could make them. Hopefully, once more, you have cheated death.

Daredevils

An absurd concept!
How could nurses dare,
even better, dare what?
Every day we lay our minds,
body, license, on the line
for a challenge, yet to see.
No canyon measured,
no cars vaulted,
no wall broached.
We still lie
on the line for
someone yet unseen.
Do we not take
the ultimate risk?
Admission to discharge.
If we don't see it,
measure it, feel it.
It is never seen.
The simple is beyond us.
To clip, remove, dissolve,
the sickness of choice.
Can I not fight, one
more time and win?
The sums multiply.
Even my patients die.
All lines stopped.
Not on my shift.
Adjust the numbers
fit the parameters
that we've agreed
meet the standards,
of what we call life.

Can we drain the body
of the poisons we gave
to keep you alive?
Before the medicine
and the sickness
overwhelm you.
Necessary Evil.
Malfunctioning.
People like me.
That could be me.
So, if you live,
then I, in effect
have denied death.
Startling awareness of my frailty.
When does my turn
come up? Who'll dare,
a nurse will be there.

09/04/92

Image

I hate the superficial
shit,
What we form our opinions
on.
See my car, my house, not
me.
For I am afraid of what you
see.
Must it be so?
We hide behind facades of
things.
Images of what we want to
be.
A collage of things, not
us,
but a picture of all our
dreams.
Pie in the sky.
For we never meet what we
would like to be, a failing soul.
Lost in a sea of photographs
screams
From a video of perceptions
scenes.
All we must have.

1/91

What is a Man

The qualities that create us
come from such varied source
that we cannot help but become
the torchbearers of individuality.
Observe those around us and
gather the cloth of ideals in folds
to conceal the fears that we feel.
Say what you mean when the
smile of dishonesty crosses lips,
tender sips of falsehood lie.
Heavy on the bearer. Listener.
I know you will not speak these.
To me, when it counts, always.
For we exchange thoughts in
kind. Knowing the intolerance
that we have learned as individuals.
For the group.

06/07/94

74

Memories of Lesser Times

I watch you fight
  the same old demons
    that you've fought before.
Age old swordplay
  in battles never won
    simply reviewed
I've fought the fight you're
  facing. I know how fast you're
    racing. There isn't always time.
You cannot break the past
  into what you will not be
    for the trap is so sublime.
What you fear the most
  will occur. You will force it.
    Scary to you, I know.
For I have felt your fear,
  because I slide into that
    which I am familiar with.
Familiar demons of youth.
  I must have it, I want it.
    And I want it now.
So in pursuit of a dream,
  line and color crystal clear,
    we find the depths of sickness.
Show me where you hurt.
  Familiar ground to me.
    Similar paths to mine.
For we must all travel
  along our chosen paths,
    just don't repeat the course.

11/14/93

Passages

Trying to fly
wings untested.
Skyward bound
As yet untested.
I was strapped
by the minds
surrounding me.
Simple finds
routed dreams
seeking travel.
Bound by tight
parental rule
constricting me.
They were fools.
I knew better,
knew it all,
I could run
and never fall.

Simple minds.
Getting stronger
found my side,
Stumbled often
break in stride.
Found some truth
some have lied,
No net yet,
still I swing,
flying blind.
I strive alone
To be someone.
Find myself
have some fun.
Is it wrong,
am I due?
Am I so different
from you?
Strength to touch

Simple thoughts
I found myself
alone on a hill.
No one around
quiet, cheap thrill.
I am proud of me,
so far of what is.
I came from you
nonsilent sacrilege
of all you hold
of an image, dream.
Of what could've been
incomplete schemer.
A matching card. from
my deck it's true.
The joker of the pack
not really fitting,
but it always comes back
Albeit unwitting.
Simple Truth.

In Respect

When faced with my own mortality
I run in fear.
Time wasted is precious.
And I withdraw inside.
So is that time also
wasted?
Time for healing
A time of cleansing
myself.

4/11/90

Death's a puzzle
they tell us.
When it's over
you get
the box.

The Noncompliant

A product of all your sins.
And I hate you!
Twelve hours of trying
to keep you from killing
yourself and me.
A posey, and restraints
and you still managed
to hit the floor.
Had to pee did you?
I can imagine after
you pulled your foley out.
Jerking off the ostomy
at 6:30 AM was cute too.
Two hours of dressing changes,
the bath, and linens, all
just shot to hell.
How did you lose
that leg? Diabetic?
Had a cut for six months
and didn't treat it.
Smoked two packs a day
for twenty years?
I know the breathing
tube is uncomfortable.
Good, deep, breaths.
About these four MI's?
How long did you wait?
Over a month of chest pain
before you came to the ER.
Piss poor protoplasm,
a burden on the system.
One I'm paying for.
Mentally and physically.
But essentially you are
still a child.

So we protect, and
watch for you
to do the stupid.
Because that is all you
have ever done.
Self destructive cycles
of denial, defeat, and
ignorance. Cycles
we must break
if health care,
as we know it,
is to survive.
So again I must
make you
walk the line.
Willing or not,
we face your future.
For some could
let you die, the
marginals, that
always have the
mysterious failures
at seven AM.
But you will not
die on me. None
are more stubborn.
So you live,
and I can sleep.

04/02/92

I wouldn't say the truth
is like a kiss.
But a kiss is what I'd like
truth to be.

Time Passing

Your eyes start to glaze
It seems just a phase
closer to ending
the silence rending
We pause
We did not fail
You did not rail
The weight of years
all consuming fears
Found you
I held your hand
A man to a man
So moments last
Thoughts that past
won't end

05/16/93

What We Are

A sudden dawning
of what we all
try to be.
A nurse is a protector,
the patient against
his body, mind.
Balancing lives is taxing
and it wears on me,
tears my heart.
It could be safe to call,
let the docs cover it.
and our asses.
But what of calls before?
False alarms when
some cry wolf?
Time for conjecture.
What could be from
what I know.
And try to look not at
the problem, but
at the person.

7/15/90

83

SHELLS

While picking up shells
on the beach today.
My eye was caught by the tip
of a magnificent conch.
An exquisite shell.
Reveling in it's perfection.
I thought "how like us"
A thousand miles of beach,
yet we all seek perfect shells.
Something better than what
we have and hold.

Yet are we all not as shells?
Born unscarred and fresh,
full of life and beauty.
To be met, sometimes marred,
or even crushed,
by the conflicts life brings us.
Cast aside by the majority
walked on as it were.
Just as we walk on the beach.
Supported by what has
come and gone before us.
The less than perfect shells.

8/25/94

WOODSTOCK VAGUELY REMEMBERED

They were different days back when Woodstock first occurred. I was twelve years old and I can still remember the fuss. Watching the kids sliding in the mud looked like tremendous fun. I think that the reason the event was really remembered was that there was the feeling of freedom surrounding the event. Listening to the promoters from the first event talk about pushing performers on stage that had no more songs to sing. Yet the songs they sang made a statement for an entire generation.

This time it seemed more for the show. Maybe as a television based society, we have become too dependent upon the entertainment value of the screen. We seek everything homogenized and pasteurized. Video phone calls, computer dating, video sex. We have become isolated from our own searches for freedom, because we never take the first step. If it was to be really good, it would have to come to us anyway. At least that is the way that the majority of us act. The unfortunate part of it is that we become dependent upon what those that acted send to us as truth. The best packaging becomes the truth.

FREEDOM

The search continues in this quest for truth.
Millions of random souls desperately uncouth.
Angry wanderers amidst those oft admired.
Still empty, but trying to bask in honors aired.
In reflected thought. Unwillingness. Defeat.

For leaders betray. Selfish as we all are.
Read the edicts passed in stone, so far.
Let someone take us. Is this freedom?
Or a box for which we are groomed?
Freedom is the ability to make the choice.

The choice is whom to believe. Receive.
Accept. Is taught to all everyday. Grieve.
For those that fail the tests accept less.
Self-pity destroys the drive to be best.
And swallows the heart inside us.

So why do some stand, eager to try?
While others merely pass the baton?
Opportunities lost by failure to act.
And the tortoise always comes back.
After beating the hare again this time.

That is freedom defined can't we see.
The positioning in the galaxy of me.
Ourselves. In what we exist in time.
Always within or without our minds.
Freedom is an action, not a goal.

8/12/94

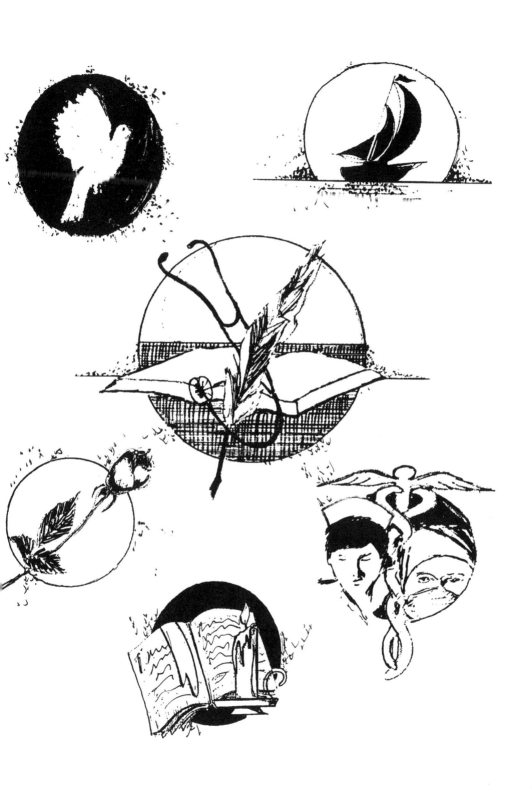

Conclusion

The healthcare system is in a state of constant change. Developing an entity that is devoted to achieving efficient, personable, effective care in a cost efficient manner is a responsibility that we can no longer afford to deny. Removing the person from the system that actually cares for the patient is not the answer to the financial question. People will always equate proper healthcare with a person at the bedside. Streamlining operations. Tracking types of illnesses. Decreasing length of stay. Patient education and family support structures. All are factors that need to be weighed in the patient survival index. The best care in the hospital is all for nothing if the rehabilitation for the patient is not carried out quickly. Then what was a salvageable human with pride and hope becomes a dependent burden on a straining system. The goal is total care for the patient. Someday we will be in the hospital. Hope someone who cares is taking care of you.